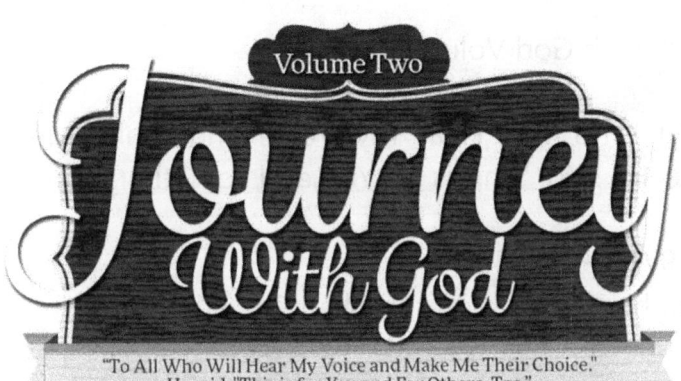

Journey with God Volume Two

"To All Who Will Hear My Voice and Make Me Their Choice. He said: "This is for You and For Others, Too."

ISBN: 978-0-9987486-6-5
Copyright © 2019 by Jesus Filled Day Publishing

All rights reserved. No part of this book may be reproduced or transmitted in any form or by any means, electronic or mechanical, including photocopying, recording, or by any information storage and retrieval system, without permission from the publisher.

Printed in the United States of America

For information contact:
Jesus Filled Day Publishing Company™
P.O. Box 34
Houston, Texas 77001
www.HaveaJesusFilledDay.com
(281) 399-4011

Dedication

I would like to dedicate this book to God above! For continually wooing me, with his mercy and love. Also to my beautiful daughter, Julie Tarver, whom the Lord gave me at a very crucial time in my life. To my son-in-law, Jason Tarver, always loving his famiy. To all my grandchildren, Jason Jr., Jacob, Joshua, and Jamilynn Tarver.

I will always be thankful to my Grandma Rawls for her standing in the gap for her family. I contribute my relationship with God because as a child she would walk me to church on Sunday mornings. Being the perfect example of what it takes to have a relationship with God.

Last, but not least, to all my family for their love.

Acknowledgment

I would like to acknowledge my husband/Pastor Roy Chapman for his love and support for me, in my ministry.

Also to Deborah Elum, whom I consider a friend and sister in the Lord. For all her hard work and prayerful support in making my book possible.

Foreword

What you hold in your hand is a treasure.
It's not a treasure of gold or silver.
It's not a treasure of money or jewels.
It's not a treasure of cars or houses or land or possessions.
What you hold in your hand is a treasure of so much more than any of those things.
It is a treasure because of what it contains.

Once again, Judy Chapman has poured out her heart, breathing life and encouragement to the reader. This second book of poems speaks to the very nature of what it means to be human and what it means to be a Christian.

These poems will allow you the chance to both smile and cry. There are times you will chuckle and times you will rest in somber silence. Sitting with some of them will cause you to inhale while sitting with others will cause you to exhale. This book isn't a filled with simple platitudes or pithy sayings. No, this is not one of those types of books. This book is so much more. It explores the highs and lows, ups and downs, and everything in between. These words speak of joy and pain, success and failure. They speak of real life. And, they speak of the real life of a Christian.

If there is one thing that I appreciate about the writing of Judy Chapman, it is the fact that I find myself unable to simply gloss over any of these words. They carry weight. They carry truth. They carry depth. They carry life. When I read these words they stay with me. They linger.

They are still on my mind hours and days after I have read them. That, my friends, is the mark of something that will last.

As you read these words, prepare to explore real life. Prepare to encounter Jesus. Prepare to continue a Journey with God.

Brock Beesley

Table of Contents

Part 1: The Son and the Spirit 13
    I Can't Say Enough 14
    Through Jesus' Name (Jesus' Blood) 15
    The Cross 17
    You Lord (You) 18
    The Intercessor 19
    Through Jesus 20
    In Jesus (I Have Received) 21
    I Am Said (He Said) 22
    Jesus Is the Answer 24
    Tried in the Fire (You) 25
    Jesus Is Coming 26
    The Heavens Proclaim (Jesus) 28
    The Spirit 29
    Holy Spirit Come (The Holy Spirit) 30
    The Holy Ghost 31

Part 2: Following Jesus 33
    Growing Up in God (I Must) 34
    Keep Your Eyes on God (Relying on God's Strength) 35
    The Enemy 36
    Satan Defeated (Put the Enemy to Flight) 37
    Lord Sometimes (Peace of Mind) 38
    Help Me Lord 39

Stay Connected to the Vine	40
Standing on a Mountain	41
I'm Standing on the Mountain	42
Jesus, A Firm Foundation	43
We, the Lost Sheep (We All, Like Lost Sheep)	45
Not Ok to Sin (Wake Up and Get Real)	47
A Life of Deceit	48
God Rules (Abide with the Savior)	49
We Must	50
Speak the Word	51
If Any Man Be In Christ (This Is the Way)	53
Today Is Mine	54
Be	55
Highway of Holiness	56
Daily in Christ (Daily)	57
I Know Jesus (I Know)	58
A Tree (A Strong Tree)	60
Tabernacle of God (The People of God)	62
Recipe for Life	63
Sand Castles	64
Going Through the Valley (The Valley)	66
Life's Road	68
Take My Hand	69
I'm Following Jesus	70
Part 3: Faith, Hope and Love	**73**
I Will Trust in the Lord	74
Choose Christ	75
Victorious Through the Valley (The Valley)	76

A Dry and Thirsty Land (Calling Us) 78
Songs in the Night 80
Abide in Jesus (Lean on Him) 82
When Trials Come 84
There Is a Stream (A Life-Flowing Stream) 85
When You Are Battle Worn (Let Jesus Pilot) 86
Victory in Jesus 87
Sometimes Alone 88
Heart to Heart Talk with Jesus (I Shall Overcome) 90
Anchored My Soul 92
Great Pain 93
Don't Worry 94
Never Fear 96
God Will (Remember God's Grace) 97
The Life Boat 98
Victory Through the Storm 100
Enjoy the Journey 101
It Is Well 102
My Testimony Story (Help Someone Today) 103
He Cares for You 105
God Will Restore 106

Part 4: Words of Wisdom 107
Understand Life 108
Deceitfulness of Riches 110
Worldly Things 111
Gossip 112
Oh Wicked Man Come Out (Repentance) 114

House Left to Its Own (A House Left to Its Own) 115
Humanity 117
When God Chooses (God's Choice) 118
A Double Minded Man (Through the Word) 119
The Gift (This Gift) 120
Power of the Tongue 121
Words 122
Thy Word 123
I've Anchored My Soul 124
The Season for Jesus 125
The Good News 126
God Is in the Wind (God Is in…) 127
Walking Along the Seashore 128
Evening Rest 129
Down in the Valley 130
A Planned Day (An Encounter with the Heavenly Host) 132
The Heart of Worship 133
The Mortal Body 134
The Times 135

Part 5: Prayer and Thanksgiving 139
Conversations with God 140
Sometimes (Sometimes I Say) 141
Communicate with God 143
On Bended Knee 144
I Come in Prayer 145
Seeking God (A Prayer to Begin Today) 146
Seek God 147
My Tears 148

 Press On 149
 Pray One for Another..150
 Lord Grant Me 151
 More of You..152
 A Time of Thanksgiving...154
 God's Plan My Mother (God's Plan).......................155

Part 6: Life, Now and to Come................................. 157
 Such a Gift (A Gift of God)......................................158
 New Life 159
 A New Song..160
 Rich in Jesus (Living for Jesus) 161
 This World Is Not My Home....................................163
 My New Home...164
 Thinking on Salvation (My Eternal Home) 165
 The Prodigal Comes Home.....................................166
 A Thing That Is Bad (God Has Prepared a Place)...167
 When I Get to Heaven...168
 I've Gone Home 169
 Call Me Gone 170
 I'm Building a City 171

Part 7: Words from God 173
 God Spoke..174
 My People...175
 Follow Me...176
 Know That I Am God..178
 I Made Everything..180
 I Will..182

Pray	183
Tell Them	184
Steal No More	185
Take Back	186
Run the Race	187
Welcome Home Child of Mine	188

Part 1: The Son and the Spirit

I Can't Say Enough

I can't say enough about Jesus.
To Him I belong.
In my heart I have a song.

He leads me in the right path.
In Him, I shall suffer no wrath.
He is my guide.
He beckons, "Follow Me.
Come inside. In Me, hide."

He delivers my soul from hell.
In Him, I can say all is well.
Of His saving power, I'm going to tell.

He cleanses me from day to day.
He's leading my way.
I'm covered by His blood.
When the enemy comes in like a flood,
He is my friend even until the end.

I am so blessed.
In Him, I take rest.

Through Jesus' Name (Jesus' Blood)

No need to cower.
Through Jesus' name we have all power.
Call on Him any day.
Any hour.

Jesus' blood sets free.
The vilest sinner can gain victory.
Free from the deepest sin
Set free from within.

God can open your eyes to deception.
He can bring correction.
God will bring the things done at night,
Exposing sin, bringing it to light.

We must be covered by His blood,
Covering our innermost being.
Like a flood, the consequences of sin.
We must make a stand
To enter the Promised Land.

Getting Egypt out of our hearts promises life.
A new start.
We must not refuse to deal with the sins in our heart.
We should seek to be hidden in Christ.
Let God take away all the dross.
Come the way of the cross.

The Cross

Jesus was acquainted with grief.
He clung to His belief
That righteousness would save.
So His life, He gave.

He came the way of the cross
So that none would be lost.
He counted it all gain,
Hanging on the cross.
He hung to an open shame
For all mankind.

Death swallowed up in victory
For all to find,
So man could say, "Victory is mine!"

You Lord (You)

Lord, You became a martyr.
You gave life-giving water.
Your soft gentle rain came washing me sane,
Taking away all pain, taking away all blame.
Letting me know and making it plain
Life's not a game.
True life is in Your name.

You didn't come seeing fortune or fame.
Your life, You gave.
Died for our sin just to seek and save
For just one who was lost.
For all, You paid the cost.
You became King of Kings,
Reconciling all things!

The Intercessor

All we like sheep have gone astray.
We have turned, everyone, to his own way.
Day after day, living life as if at play.

The Lord hath laid on Him the iniquity of us all,
Reconciling the fall.
He hath poured out His soul unto death,
Unto man breathing new life from His breath.

He was numbered with the transgressors.
He bore the sin of many.
Made intercession for transgression
So there would be no regression
Being made whole, new life to our soul.
The intercessor became bold.
Our future Jesus does hold.

He overcame sin that we could enter in.
New life had begun
Through Jesus, God's son.
In the end, victory has been won!

Through Jesus

Through Jesus' ascension came redemption.
Men stood in awe
As he was being released from the curse of the law.
No more sting of death
As Jesus His last breath.

He hath raised us up with Him.
The enemy now was condemned.
Having all authority, Jesus and I agree.
The bound shall be set free.
Healed.
Through the cross Salvation was revealed.
It was sealed.

In Jesus (I Have Received)

The true Word of God
I have received.
In Jesus,
I know whom I have believed.
The Spirit of God
In me has been conceived.
And at last
My soul is relieved.

I Am Said (He Said)

I searched and I searched
But I could not find no joy.
No peace would come to mind.

I prayed to the Savior, "Please Lord comfort me."
He said, "I've come to give you life
And that more abundantly."

He opened my eyes so that I could see His love,
Ever so gentle engulfing me, picking me up.
He placed me on this rock,
Whispering, "I hear My sheep when they knock."
His voice, so strong and true,
"I'll never leave nor forsake you.
I'll always be here for you."
His voice so piercing, "I've opened thy ears.
Come follow Me. I'll give length of years."

Speaking so true and firm within me,
My heart did yearn.
He said, "I call thee Mine.
I come to seek.

I'll leave the ninety and nine.
I'll bear you up on angel's wings,
Bringing you home as all heaven sings."

Jesus Is the Answer

Jesus is the answer for you and me today.
He is the only way.
He is the answer to all our needs.
We must give account for all our deeds.

Jesus is the key for all humanity.
We must put away all vanity.
He unlocks the door forevermore.
The answer to eternal life and so much more,
He is the Door!

Tried in the Fire (You)

You are The Potter and I am the clay.
You are molding and shaping me each day.

When you put me in the fire
Your plan is my desire.
I will have faith and pray to do things Your way,
Come what may.
You, I'll trust,
Realizing it's a must,
Knowing You are the Creator who formed me from the dust.

You are all powerful and all knowing,
Leading and guiding my path, showing.
As the clay is in the Potter's hand,
You shape and hold,
Trying me in the fire as pure gold.
And one day, Your face to behold.

Jesus Is Coming

Jesus is coming in the power of His might.
The enemy must take flight.
He knows he has lost the fight.

Jesus is coming to claim His own,
Preparing the way in the wilderness,
Bringing His people home,
Never more to roam.

He's coming to deliver and set free
The captives who have been bound.
They must bow their knee.

I Am, He is coming back.
Restoring, even as the enemy is roaring,
Trying to devour every hour.
In the name of Jesus he must cower.
He must run.
His fate has already been done.
He is a defeated foe.
In the name of Jesus he must go!

Jesus has all power.
We can call on Him any hour.
He is King of Kings,
Ruler over all living things.
He is the giver of life and all that is good.
He makes right, gives songs in the night.
Jesus makes everything right.
He knows no sin.
Jesus is where it all began.

The Heavens Proclaim (Jesus)

In Jesus name the heavens proclaim!
Sent to earthen vessels, never to be the same.

God ordained Your name.
Bright and Morning Star!
What a Wonderful Counselor You are.

You light up the darkest of night,
Shining so bright,
Coming in the power of Your might!

Shaping the clay day after day,
Leading and guiding, showing the way.
Coming back after the Bride, a wife.
Touched by the Spirit, giving life.
You are the Potter.
Shape and mold!
So, one day Your face I shall behold.

The Spirit

He came from above,
Revealing His love in the form of a dove.
Sealing us into His kingdom come,
His will to be done.

Calling us sons of God,
Our hearts He did prod.
Planting us in His rich sod to set us free,
Giving life and that more abundantly,
To live eternally.

Holy Spirit Come (The Holy Spirit)

The natural man does not receive the things of God.
They are foolishness to Him,
Nor can he know them.

The Holy Spirit sets the believer free
To be what God intended for Him to be.
His Word saves through the washing and renewing of our mind.
Only then, true peace you can find.

His Spirit causes us to walk with God
And on serpents trod.
Knowing the Lord is our Shepherd,
We will not want.
No good thing will He withhold.

In the Word, speaking, being bold.
The Holy Spirit, a transforming power.
Any day, any hour.
His Spirit from on high.
God, coming nigh.

The Holy Ghost

What the enemy has noosed
The Dove has loosed!
Setting free from sin
Giving new life within.
Letting new life begin.

There is no limit
When the Holy Ghost is in it.

The Holy Ghost is given for inspiration,
Birthed through creation.
It's the Breath of Life to encourage,
To have courage.
No more low self-esteem.
Just Holy Ghost power to redeem.

Part 2: Following Jesus

Growing Up in God (I Must)

To grow up in my salvation,
I must remember God is the author and finisher of all creation
I must crave pure spiritual food,
Not let circumstances control my mood.

I must put on the whole armor of God,
Desiring the Word to nourish my soul, even until I am old.
I must desire it more than food or drink,
Never letting my faith sink,
Realizing that life is more important than fleshly things this life brings.

Keeping my eyes on the prize, getting wisdom and understanding,
Letting God give me spiritual eyes.
I must feast on God's Word,
Hearing His voice, knowing He can be heard,
Being still and know that He is God.

I must partake at His table,
Feeding on His Word.
In the end, I am well able.

Keep Your Eyes on God
(Relying on God's Strength)

Through our weakness we are made strong,
Relying on God's strength all the day long.
And looking back, seeing how far we have gone.
Yes, closer to Him, closer to our goal.
Detouring sin. Detouring Sheol.

To Him, sold out.
Standing on the Word without doubt,
Being sons and daughters of the Most High.
Always through prayer, drawing nigh,
Covered by His blood from God on high.
Of His saving grace, we testify.

The Enemy

The enemy goes to and fro upon the earth
Seeking whom He may devour.
Pray in the Spirit.
Seek God.
Walk in His power.

Praying in the Spirit,
Walking in His might,
Putting the enemy to flight.
The enemy will cower.
Through His Word, he has no power.

In Jesus, your life is complete.
Through the Word, the enemy, you can defeat,
Putting him under your feet.

Satan Defeated (Put the Enemy to Flight)

What Jesus did at the cross was completed.
Satan is defeated.

Satan's ploy is to destroy,
To take away your joy.
I must confess He wants to oppress,
Depress, bring unrest, destroy God's best.
He does constantly attack.
Wants you to suffer lack.

He is a deceiver.
Don't be a receiver.
Be a believer!
Believe and speak the Word.
Let it be heard.
Your mind, gird.
Walk in the power of God's might,
Not by sight.
Fight the good fight.
Put the enemy to flight.

Lord Sometimes (Peace of Mind)

Sometimes I find I have no peace of mind.
I can't find any rest.
Lord, I know it's because I haven't given You my best.
I've invited the enemy in as my guest.
Listening to his lies, I should know his scheme.
It's to destroy, not to redeem.
The enemy should not be entreated.
He should be put under our feet, defeated.

Then, I'm fully aware of my despair.
I go to God in prayer.
He's always there.
Then, I find
I have peace of mind.

Help Me Lord

Precious Lord, take me by the hand.
Help me stand.
Help me obey Your command,
Leading me into the Promised Land.
Give me peace and faith to obey,
No matter what come what may.

Place Your seal.
Give me zeal.
Strength to do Thy will.

A voice for Jesus proclaimed.
A vessel of honor that needeth not be ashamed,
Placing my feet on solid ground.
Desire with God's saints to hang around.
Praising and giving God the glory,
Proclaiming the salvation story.

Stay Connected to the Vine

To sin, we should not be a slave.
To us, God's Son He gave
That we should gain victory over death, Hell and the grave.
Our ears, we must incline.
Stay connected to the vine,
When we trust in the Word, the Divine!

"Come nigh. I am He.
I cannot lie.
Be rooted and grounded in the Word.
I set free.
Come, follow Me.
Live eternally."

Standing on a Mountain

I'm standing on a mountain.
There is a valley I see.
I know that valley can't conquer me.

I'm standing on a solid foundation.
The solid rock I see
And Jesus is the key.
Though the mountain be great or small
I cannot fall for I'm heeding Jesus call.

I'm standing on a mountain no man can climb.
I have been carried by the Divine.
I'll not be left behind.

I'm standing on a mountain.
I've found Jesus to be mine.

I'm Standing on the Mountain

I'm standing on the mountain,
Drinking from the heavenly fountain.
Jesus is restoring my soul.

He has taken away my valleys
And in Him, I am now bold.
It's victory in Jesus,
More precious than gold.
I have a story.
It's one that must be told.

My feet are dancing and I know it won't be long.
Jesus is leading me on my way home.
I'm praising my Savior for I'm never alone.
And one day I'll be standing around God's throne
Where I belong in my heavenly home.
I'm standing on a mountain following Christ,
The risen King, for He is my everything.

Jesus, A Firm Foundation

Satan has many devices,
Sends many vices.
He sends a counterfeit and strong delusion.
It's only an illusion.
His way is sinking sand.
It's all in His plan,
Disabling man where he can't stand.
Sometimes painting a pretty picture,
It's only a restrictor.

Jesus is the rock on which I stand.
Living life grand, Jesus plan for man.
Honoring God in all His ways,
The man that loves God prays.
He shall prolong his days.
He gives correction.
He gives direction and discretion.
He gives this man the desires of his heart.
His love He shall impart.

He never leaves nor forsakes.
He will never depart.

Give Him your whole heart, building on a firm foundation,
Gaining eternal life for the duration.

We, the Lost Sheep
(We All, Like Lost Sheep)

For one another, we should pray harder.
Longer. More sincere.
For all God's children are precious and dear.

To God, we should draw near.
We all, like lost sheep have gone astray.
Wandering aimlessly day after day.
The Shepherd urges, "Draw near to Me."
Seek Me while I may be found
And you will abound."
Not one jot nor tittle shall fall to the ground.

For all shall stand in the judgement
And give account for his life
We must be covered by Jesus blood.
From our life, remove strife.

In the multitude of counselors there is wisdom.
Living for God, there is freedom. Remove sin.
Come by the way of the cross. Enter in.

Don't judge. Don't begrudge.
Love one another. Love your brother.
One another's burdens, bear.
For one another, be there. Care.
"When you've done it unto the least of these
You've done it as unto Me.
Obey My commands. I set free.
Come unto Me."

Not Ok to Sin (Wake Up and Get Real)

If you think it's ok to go to church
And lie, cheat and steal
You had better wake up and get real,
And for God get some zeal!
Let Jesus heal.
Sin does nothing but kill.

Here is some advice:
Don't let the enemy get you into a vice.
Repent.
Turn to Jesus before your life has been spent.
To the lost He was sent.
It's not ok to willfully sin.
To get your heart right, ask Jesus in.
Let new life begin.

A Life of Deceit

Living a life of deceit
Is living a life of defeat.

Deceit is living a lie
And God's command You deny.
Deceit is living in vain,
Living a life of pain, playing a game.
Deceit is not being truthful to the inner man,
For this was not in God's plan.

God is truth. He doesn't change.
He's always the same.
Walk in truth. Call on Jesus name.
God's Word, keep.
Choose life, not deceit.

God Rules (Abide with the Savior)

God rules and pays His dues.

"There is reaping and sowing,
Assuredly knowing You are mine.
I am thine,
And Satan wants to render you blind.
He wants to take over your mind.

He wants to cheat you, beat you like a child
He wants to run and hide."
Trusting in God's Word and speaking it, we can abide
With the Savior with arms open wide.
He is the same yesterday, today and tomorrow.
He adds no sorrow to them that believe.
Peace that passes all understanding, you receive.

We Must

We must all come to the altar lest we falter.
We must count the cost lest we be lost.
We must have a change of heart.
Then only does new life start.
We must read God's Word,
And for Him hunger and thirst,
Putting Him first.
We must love God with our whole heart.
Give God all our trust, we must!

Speak the Word

Just when we think everything is fine
And we're walking around on cloud nine,
So to speak,
We soon realize without the Word we're weak.

Jesus is the Word.
We must speak the Word
If we want to be heard.
We must be wise to Satan's lies.

He has many schemes to tear down our dreams.
He has mistreated.
Speaking the Word leaves him as he is: defeated.
He has used and abused God's children.
He has confused.

Reading the Word lets us know God is real
And God implants much zeal,
Which lets us know God has placed His seal.
Speaking the word is a verb.

Action equals reaction.
Extraction equals Satan equals history.
Jesus equals victory.
No end. Life everlasting.
At the cross Jesus came to seek and save the lost.
He paid the cost!

If Any Man Be In Christ (This Is the Way)

If any man be in Christ He is a new creature.
Old things are passed away.
Leaving hurts and problems behind,
You'll find it's a new day.
This is the way.
Walk ye in it.
Your life will benefit.
Remember, for you all things have become new!

We must forgive if for God we want to live.
Remember, He forgave you.
It's one of God's commands He demands. Forgive.
Have life more abundantly. Live.
If the enemy is eating away at your heart,
Confess your sins. Get a new start.
Grace, God will impart.
If you don't forgive you can't be forgiven.
Forgiveness is why Jesus has risen.
In the end, eternal life given.

Today Is Mine

Today is mine.
Living for Jesus, the devil I bind.
Perfect peace I find,
No longer by the flesh confined.
Walking in the Spirit.
Free from sin because I let Jesus in,
Letting new life begin,
Jesus living within.

He's my friend.
Praising His name until the end.

Be

Be of sound speech that cannot be condemned,
That he that is contrary may be ashamed.
Of a rebellious nature, be not blamed.
In all things showing thyself a pattern of good works.

Be sincere.
Be an ambassador for Christ. Draw near,
Being of sound mind, never living in fear.
Be honest. Speak evil of no man.
Be gentle. Show all meekness to all men
Every time you can.

Highway of Holiness

There is a highway.
It's one of holiness.
For one to overcome,
It's where the race is to be run.

The highway is called straight.
It's His gate.
Lay aside every weight
That does so easily beset thee.
Remember it is He.
Without, no man can see God.
Seek His face no matter where thy feet trod.

Let God lead and guide.
He'll walk by your side,
If in Him you confide.
Enter the narrow gate.
Make yourself ready.
He'll make your feet steady.
In Him, hide.
Come, be part of the bride.

Daily in Christ (Daily)

I am in Christ and Christ is in me.
This is how it must be for me to live eternally.
My sight is set on Thee.

My attitude must be gratitude.
Above all, servitude.
I daily seek to be cleansed of sin.
In my life, letting Jesus in.
Daily, seeking the will of God.
Through my behavior,
Letting the world know Jesus is my Savior!

I must accept God's ongoing rescuing,
Delivering power every hour, remembering
It's not by might, nor by power,
But through Jesus Spirit.
Only then Satan can't devour.
I must trust Jesus to save,
Remembering for me His life, He gave.

I Know Jesus (I Know)

I know through the blood of Jesus I have victory.
I know against me Satan has an assignment.
I know when I plead the blood
My body, soul and spirit will come into alignment.
I know Thy Word is a lamp unto my feet.
I know in the Word I shall not suffer defeat.
I know Jesus is able to keep.

I know Satan is a master at lying and deceit.
I know Jesus. Satan is under my feet.
I know there is no temptation that can bring separation.
I know Satan is a defeated foe.
This, I know.

I know in Jesus I shall prosper and be in good health.
Of sound mind, eyes that see and not blind.
I know these things I shall find.
I know in the Word I have Jesus mind.
I know I shall not turn back nor be discouraged on my journey.
I know I can go to Jesus. He's my attorney.
I know in Him the weak can say, "I'm strong."

I know living for Jesus I can't go wrong.
I know in Jesus the path is made straight.
I know my way to heaven.
Jesus will lead me to Thy gate.

A Tree (A Strong Tree)

It's no strange thing to me
That Jesus would say be a strong, strong tree.
Jesus hung and died for thee
And in three days he rose in victory.
He paid the price for the tree.

To me, it's no strange thing.
We must bend our knee.
A strong, strong tree.
"This is what you can be as you grow up in Me:
One whose branches reach out into the sea
Giving shelter to those who are lost, needing to be set free;
One whose roots go deep into the earth.
Rooted and grounded in Me,
Bringing to life much worth, bearing much fruit."
Through life's storms, extending sheltering arms.
One that stands tall and trim
Extending much light in the darkness of night,
Helping others draw close to Him.

The Most High God, leading and guiding
As He is providing,
Giving shade from the sweltering heat to those in need.
Given to feed,
Given to charity, bringing clarity.
It's the tree of life, staying close to the Most High God.
Setting your roots into rich sod.
Fertilized by the trials of life
Overcoming, not given to strife.
Growing in love, bring about eternal life.
Removing all doubt to those without.
Extending love, for love covers a multitude of sins.
This is where life begins,
Being a tree, being set free.
Life eternally.

Tabernacle of God (The People of God)

The tabernacle of God is with men.
The voice of God sends His word, "Enter in."
He will dwell with them.
The light comes from Him.
They shall be His people for He is their God.
Having the preparation of the Gospel their feet shod.

In Him, there is no fear.
He is their God.
He draws near.
He shall wipe away thy tear.
Incline thine ear.
For they shall not have lived in vain
And there shall be no pain.
The former things have passed away.
There'll be no more night, only day.

"For I Am the Truth and the Way,
The Alpha and Omega, the beginning and the end."
These are those who have made themselves ready
Which do His commands,
Trusting in Jesus, putting their life in God's hands.

Recipe for Life

In a huge bowl for all to behold,
Mix in an overabundance of heaping tablespoons of love.
Fold in the brand sent from above.

Sweeten with pure scoops of God's grace
So that I may look upon His Face.

Mix thoroughly lots of forgiveness.
Stirring until I'm in the direction of doing God's business.
Grate in some gest
To run life's race and give it my best
That I may enter into God's rest.

Mix in thoroughly faith, never giving in to defeat.
Pour me overflowing into a baking sheet
So I can spread God's love to everyone I meet.

Cover with Jesus blood. God's Son.
Bake until well done!

Instructions: recipe for life should be baked until
"Well done my good and faithful servant."

Sand Castles

Sand castles can't stand
Even though you build them grand.
Sand castles are not real.
God promises the enemy comes to tear down and steal,
For God's laws are real.

For Him, we must have much zeal,
Building your house on the sand
When the rough waves of life come.
They will.
It can't stand when the rain comes.
It washes it away.
So build your house on the rock today.

It rains on the just and unjust.
In God we must put all our trust.
For if we love house, land, father, mother, sister or brother
More than Jesus we are not fit for the Kingdom of God.
We must not live in the land of nod.
We must awake from our sleep.
God's Word, built in our lives deep.
His commands, keep.

When God sends a test,
We must build our house to the best,
Knowing when trouble comes we can rest.

And, remember sand castles will wash away.
We must pray.
Build on the solid rock.
So when the rains come and the winds blow,
In Jesus, we know our life will abound on solid ground.
Still be around.

Going Through the Valley (The Valley)

Down in the valley where the green grass grows
There's life-giving water from the Master that flows.
Where the grass is so green,
Words from the Father we're able to glean.
A place of learning.
A place of yearning,
Washed in His fountains,
Able to climb mountains.

A place where we're made clean
And we know He does redeem.
Only then unseen things can be seen.

So, down in the valley never dread.
It's a place where the living are being made overcomers.
It's not for the dead.
A place for the Father to give thy daily bread.
A place to make thy Father thy head.
A place to receive thy life-giving water.
A place of sustaining and in Him remaining.

Going through the valley in faith.
Never complaining,
Walking through the valley.
It's life's highway.
You can meet angels unaware in the byway.
In the valley you can hear Jesus say,
"Come My way, the way of the cross.
I am Master of the day."

Life's Road

When on life's road we carry a heavy load,
Burdened down, the enemy hanging around.
Then, there comes a sound.
The sound of victory.
A voice calling, "Come unto Me."
A voice calling from the deep
Saying, "I promise to keep.
Wake from thy sleep."

He's leading to the path called straight.
Beckoning, "Enter My gate."
There'll be roadblocks.
Then, faith knocks.
Beckoning, leading home,
No more to roam.

Take My Hand

Lord, take my hand.
Lead me by the power of Your right hand,
Leading me to the Promised Land.
On holy ground, let me stand.

Bless me with boldness in Your Word,
Guiding my steps,
Taking me to greater depths.
Set my tongue on fire to speak the Word with bold face.
Make my calling sure to run this race.

Plant Your Word into the deepest part of my being.
Give me a love for my fellow man.
Holding Your hand,
Being my brother's keeper and a God seeker,
Being stronger in the Word and faith.
Never weaker.

For when I am weak, I am made strong through faith,
leading me home.

I'm Following Jesus

I'm following Jesus each moment.
Each day
I must come the way of the cross.
He's leading me that way,
Being led by the Spirit.
He is the Divine,
Leading and guiding one step at a time.
Hearing His call,
"I am Thine and you are mine."

I have invited Jesus inside.
In Him, I shall abide.
I'll continue to knock.
He is the solid rock that's higher than I.
He never leaves nor forsakes.
He never denies.

As He leads me on,
I'll enjoy my journey home.
Victorious, I'm coming out.

I'll leave with a shout.
When I think of tomorrow I have no sorrow
because He's in control.
And one day His face I shall behold.

Part 3: Faith, Hope and Love

I Will Trust in the Lord

I will trust in the Lord.
Not in part, to Him I will pour out my heart.
God is a refuge unto me.
From the depths of my heart I cry unto Thee.

I trust in the Lord, for faith to see
Great riches and spiritual blessings You give unto me.
Thy lovingkindness is better than life.
I will continually praise Thee.

My soul shall be satisfied.
By you, justified.
Giving thanks for the rest of my days,
Giving the Lord praise.
In all my ways will I trust

Choose Christ

It is Christ we must choose.
Without repentance, we lose.

We must persevere while we are here.
Be ready to serve and God will preserve.
The enemy, we must, through the Word, put Him under our feet
In order to defeat.

Unto Him, submitting to His plan.
This is the will for man.

To Him be the glory.
This must be our life story

Victorious Through the Valley (The Valley)

I know I have a Savior without a doubt.
I come out of the valley with a loud shout.
Through this valley, victorious I came out!

I know whence I came.
I'll never be the same.
In the valley I only had to call on His name.

Praise the Lord.
He carried me through.
I see more clearly.
I feel new.

For my experience, no need to feel blue.
Though the path seemed dark and bleak,
His face, I had only to seek.
Though meek, I stood bold.
I'm more than a conqueror.

In the Bible I'm told His word is true.
Through the valley, He'll carry you through.
So, your giants, pursue.
With singing and shouting
You can come out victorious, too.

A Dry and Thirsty Land (Calling Us)

Before me a dry and thirsty land I see.
It's as dry as can be.
There's no rain in sight.
The rain has taken flight.
There are cracks on the ground,
Scare pools of water around.
Not much vegetation to be found.
There are signs of a drought.

There are signs that say pray for rain today.
But when I look into the skies, in my demise,
I think of God, how majestic and wise,
Looking with His eternal eyes.
Mindful of men, it's all in His plan.
Sending a drought because God's ways we are without.

Calling us back to Himself saying "Seek Me while it is day."
Beckoning, "Pray. I'll bring restoration your way.
I'll lead you through green pastures.
I'll restore your soul," as in the Word we're told.
Could it be He's beckoning?
Take back what the enemy has stole.

Calling us to holiness, "Repent. Confess."
Without these things no man shall see God.
Could it be He's beginning to prod,
Saying "I'll give you rest.
For you I gave My best.
When the day is done remember I gave you My Son,
That the earth may drink of this living water.

Again, never to thirst, and with life the earth would burst.
I replenish. I am Alpha and Omega.
It is finished."

Songs in the Night

Songs in the night speaking.
Seeking.
Songs in the night put the enemy to flight.
The weight of my burdens become light,
Letting me know I don't walk by sight.

I know Jesus is by my side.
He's beckoning, "In Me, hide.
I'll carry you when you are weak and can't see your way through.
Again, I say I'll carry you.

Lean on Me.
Lean heavily.
I'll give you joy for your tears.
I'll add length of years.
I'll even send laughter, joy ever after."

Songs in the night shall be your plight.
In the power of My might you'll not walk by sight.
Songs in the night give refuge from the fight,
soothing thee.
Everything is going to be alright."

Songs in the night, visited by God's own Son.
Blessed assurance, victory has been won.
"Lean on Me. Sing the song of victory!"
His blood covers eternally.

Abide in Jesus (Lean on Him)

Don't give up.
Seek God.
Let Him fill your cup.
Let Him fill it to the full.
Don't give in to the enemy's pull.

Keep on trudging.
Life's problems, never be grudging.
They are to make you grow,
Causing you to lean on Jesus
So that Him you would know,
Causing you to love Him more.

He's beckoning.
Step into the water.
Leave the shore.
He's teaching you faith and trust.
In order to please God, these we must.

So, lean on Him.
He is the light and it's not by might.
He's our guide and in Him we must abide.
We must repent of sin and in Jesus confide
Before we can enter heaven and hear,
"Welcome friend. Come inside."

When Trials Come

When trials come we must not complain,
But call on Jesus' name,
Never taking God's name in vain.
When God's name we profane,
You're playing the enemy's game.

Your faith, He has come to destroy.
God's love you must employ.
Through your trials count it all joy.
Praise God, as your trials you go through.
Stand back and watch how He'll elevate you.
Trials are to make you wiser and stronger and establish your steps,
Taking you to greater depths.

So, when trials come don't act dumb.
Remember life is a race that must be run.
Run as a servant of God, a workman that needeth not be ashamed
Let it be said, God's name you have not profaned.
In Him, victory over trials, claimed.

There Is a Stream (A Life-Flowing Stream)

In the desert there is a life-flowing stream.
God's strength to glean when to Jesus you cling.
Giving light in the darkest of night,
Shining so bright in the power of His might.

Never living in defeat,
Going through the battle never having to retreat.
Never being battle worn,
From every wind of doctrine being torn.

Always knowing whence thy strength comes from,
Having thine eyes open in wisdom.
Strength for thy journey to come,
Mounting up on strength of eagles' wings,
As thy will be done.

By His power, to run victorious in the Spirit of His might.
To overcome, 'till His will be done.

When You Are Battle Worn (Let Jesus Pilot)

Let Jesus pilot your storm.
Let grace and mercy pilot thee
Over life's stormy sea.
And when the winds of life blow,
In faith, onward go.

When the waves rise high,
Speak the Word.
Look the enemy in the eye.
Tell him God is your supply.

Let Jesus pilot thee.
On bended knee, He'll be your compass
Though the sea doth rage and roar.
Jesus will take you to the shore.

Victory in Jesus

For every disappointment God sends His ointment,
The healing Balm of Gilead.
It's called, "The City of Glad."
It's where peace in God can be had.

Every discouraging word has been heard.
There is help on the way,
For God has the last say.
With God, sup.
Fill your cup to overflowing in His truth,
Knowing there is victory in Jesus.

Sometimes Alone

Sometimes we must walk alone,
Trust Jesus as we journey on.
Sometimes we must lose in order to gain,
Trusting in Jesus.
Our life hasn't been lived in vain.

So, keep your eyes on Jesus, my friend.
He's one unto the end.
A friend indeed to the one in need.
The Word says, "Eye hath not seen.
Ear hath not heard.
Nor has it entered into the heart of man
What God has in store."
Yes, He has so much more.

So, walk alone if you must.
In Jesus, trust.
He changes not.
Everything you have need of He's got!
He owns it all.

So, if alone stand firm and tall.
He'll catch you when you fall.
He's the great I am.
All in All.
King of Kings.
He owns all things!

Heart to Heart Talk with Jesus (I Shall Overcome)

Lord, I don't know what You are doing.
But, You are the one in control.
I thought I knew what my day would hold.
But, I've had to pack my bags
And go to another job.
Yes, I began to sob.

I began to speak, "The enemy is not going to rob me of my joy!"
Your love You did employ.
I began to speak, "My God is in control
His face I will behold."

I will rise up and be the head and not the tail.
I will prevail.
When I'm weak I'll say I'm strong.
When the enemy begins to knock
I'll stand on the rock.

I'll lean on God's grace
Seeking His face and say, "All is well.
God won't leave my soul in hell."

I shall overcome.
My race, I shall run.

Anchored My Soul

Though the tempest rage and jest,
I have anchored my soul in the haven of rest.
I'm in Jesus bosom.
I'm His guest.
I am blessed.
He hideth my soul in the depths of His love.
From satan's rages, I'm far above.

There's no need to worry.
No need to hurry,
From the Word of God, I'm told.
Speak the Word in faith.
Be bold.

Through this trial I'll walk it out in faithful shout.
Through it all a child of the King, revealed.
Of all fear, healed.
In the name of Jesus I've been sealed!

Great Pain

Great pain can make a man insane.
And sometimes he goes about
Searching for someone to blame.
In great pain there can be great gain.
It teaches us this world and the lust thereof
Never stays the same.

We must trust in our creator.
Better sooner than later.
Pain makes us grow
And know God loves us so.

God wants us to turn to Him in our every need,
Never to worldly lusts and greed.
All else is sinking sand.
On this solid rock we must stand.
He knows what we have need of before we ask.
For Him, it is no task.
In His mercy, we must bask.

Don't Worry

Bring everything to God in prayer.
Be anxious for nothing.
Remember in your troubles,
God is there.
Go to Jesus.
When you are tired and worn,
He can calm the storm.

Don't let the enemy discourage.
Be of good courage.
No more worry.
No more hurry.
Worry can't add anything good to your life.
Only strife.
Worry will make you sick.
Read the Word.
Let it convict.

Your emotions, let the Savior heal.
Don't let the enemy rob or steal.
God's grace is sufficient for everyday,
In every way.

Worry is not of God.
A good man's steps are ordered by the Lord,
Wherever they may trod.
No more worry.
Follow God.

Never Fear

Never fear.
God is near.

The enemy tries to put fear in your mind,
Sometimes as if on rewind.
He's cruel, never kind.
Fear, you must overcome.
Put the enemy on the run.

Get your Bible out.
The Word, shout!
Through the Word, attack fear.
In faith, know Jesus is near.

God Will (Remember God's Grace)

When life's deserts you face,
Remember God's grace.
Streams of life-giving water,
This He will give to you.
He'll refresh and renew.
This God promises and He will do.

As we walk in faith,
Look life's struggles and disappointments in the face.
Stand up and take our place.
Make up our minds and run this race.
After all, we're born again believers which makes us receivers.
Born again, from the curse of sin.
Born of a royal priesthood.
If this, we could only understand!

We're strangers in this land.
But God promises to lead and guide,
If in Him, we'll confide.
His face He'll never hide.

The Life Boat

My eyes are fixed on Jesus.
In the life boat I now reside,
For in Jesus I now abide.
He's taking me on a journey to a far country,
One I've never seen before.
I'm following Jesus, in whom I adore.
He's giving me life and so much more.

My treasures are laid up in heaven.
I can hear Him say, "Follow Me."
He's bidding me, "Launch out into the deep."
I can see it's clear sailing.
My future, He's unveiling.
He's speaking, "I'm able to keep.
My way, seek."

I've found that narrow path that leads to salvation,
For I'm in the life boat.
It will take me to my destination.
It's truth for any situation.
My eyes are on Jesus, in whom I trust.
He's making my way clear.
He's very near.

As I sail through the rough sea He speaks to me.
He is my guide.
In Him, I prayerfully confide
As I enter into His rest,
Knowing He gives His best
He's taking my hand,
Leading me to the Promised Land.
I shall bid this world goodbye.
He shall split the eastern sky
In the twinkling of an eye.

Victory Through the Storm

Over the horizon storm clouds are appearing
And danger is nearing.
I have no fear.
I know my Jesus is near.
He'll give me strength to endure
Until the sky is clear.

Though the storm may linger long,
Jesus won't guide me wrong.
I have faith He will guide me safely home.
To me, no harm shall come
Until my journey is done.

My race, in victory I will have run.
Then, eternal life will have begun.
I shall see Jesus, God's only Son.
The crown of life, I will have won!

Enjoy the Journey

Enjoy the journey.
Keep this one thing in mind: look up.
There's no mountain too high to climb.
There's no mountain so steep,
No valley too deep Jesus is able to keep.
There's nothing He won't do.
He'll carry you through.

Your journey, walk on through.
He'll make it clear.
He's always near.
It's a journey full of mercy and grace.
Run the race.
It's a journey with no end.

It Is Well

It is well with my soul.
Jesus will be with me
Through days of old.
Victory through Jesus, as pure gold.
I'll come through the fire, tried!
I'll not be denied.

It is well.
Victory over death and hell.
It is well.
The story of Jesus, I'm going to tell.
It is well.
Jesus has set me free,
Life eternally!

My Testimony Story
(Help Someone Today)

Our life has a story to tell
And we would do well
As we journey down the road
Seeing a man with a heavy load, indeed
God's voice we should heed

When we see someone in need
Saying a little prayer along the way
Asking God, "How can we help someone today?"
For someone, we could be there,
Answering their prayer
so he, too, can say
"God sent a man my way."
He can give thanks and pray
And ask what could he do for someone today?

Each day we shouldn't waste or live in haste
Giving God all the praise for length of days
Acknowledging Him in all our ways.

There is no telling what our life could entail.
Living for God is living life well.
I am giving God all the credit and glory.
This is my testimony story.

In my time of need, it was a blessing to all who were involved.
God is with us in the good and the bad times, I am resolved.

He Cares for You

When you don't know what to do
God will make a way for you.

Just remember Jesus paid the cost
So that none would be lost.
He died for our sin
So heaven we can enter in.

When it seems all hope is gone
And everything is going wrong
Go to God in prayer.
He'll always meet you there.
You'll find you're always on His mind.
He really does care.

God Will Restore

Giving our lives over to Him, counting the cost
God is restoring all that is lost
He's repairing the despairing
Repairing broken things
As He redeems.

Never giving in, saying no to sin.
Given to win.
Opening the door to righteousness
Letting Jesus come in
Letting Him be our friend.

He will restore, give us much more.
We can't comprehend what He has in store
If we'll let Him in.
We only need to open the door.
He'll restore.
We'll be complete.
Our needs He will meet.
We'll put the enemy under our feet!

God will restore.

Part 4: Words of Wisdom

Understand Life

There are some who don't regard life.
And when I speak of life I mean eternal life.
In some men's eyes they think they are wise.
They really don't understand their demise.
They trust in financial success.
They don't care about the rest.

There are some things money can't buy.
The things that really count you can't mount.
For to love is far above what man can understand or see,
Except God would show thee.
For to care, share and love
Is a gift that can only come from above.
For it's not in things that this life brings.
They are only to use,
Not something to worry if you should lose
A life is to be treasured
And not measured according to the world's standards.

I say pay attention to wisdom, understanding and love.
Only these things bring life. Only then strife ceases,
Which releases the lies and ties that bind.
So I say care, share and walk in love.
Then, you will find you'll be guided by God
While upon this earth You trod.

Deceitfulness of Riches

Eternal life is not in things
That this life brings.
For the deceitfulness of riches
Have dug many ditches.
And the cares of the world
Will take you down to the pit.
For the Kingdom
Will render you unfit.

In things, do not lust.
In Jesus only, trust.

Worldly Things

Seeking riches sometimes leads us into ditches.
Worldly things is not all it seems.
Peace and happiness, it never brings.

We work hard for wealth.
It destroys our health.
It's as if we live in a fog.
Through life, we wallow as the hog.

Ever learning,
Never coming to the knowledge of who God is.
Never being doers of the Word,
Having ears but we've never heard.

Through life having eyes but we do not see.
Worldly things and this world do not give life eternally.
Only through Jesus can this be.

Sin, we must not condone
Until we reach our eternal home.
Pray until the day.

Gossip

I've heard people say gossip is cheap.
But on the other hand I say it cuts deep.
It's ploy is to destroy.
The person who lets Satan use them,
Like a tool, is being a fool.
I pray that God deliver me of such a way.
Lord help me not to succumb, but to overcome.
I've done it many times before
And I pray I do it no more.
Because, if I don't love the person I've seen,
The Word of God says, "How can I love God whom I've never seen?"

God is love.
This is His command: "Love one another."
This will be the one who stands and shall see God.
We must get the beam out of our own eye
Or we will die.
We need to rid ourselves of strife
So we may inherit eternal life.

I say refuse to be used.
Satan has abused God's children too long!
I say gossip no more. It's wrong.
We must be rooted and grounded in God's Word.
So, let it be said and heard.
So I beseech, be a builder of the breach!

Oh Wicked Man Come Out (Repentance)

Wicked men must repent
Before their life is spent.
They must turn to God's Word.
Realize their life is absurd.
They are living in dread among the dead.
They need to read the Word to cleanse their head.

They should pray with all their might
Before they lay down at night.
Seek what is right.
Because, as a man thinketh so is he.
He needs Jesus to gain the victory.
He has to hear Jesus voice saying, "Come unto Me.
Let Me set you free.

Come, the way of the cross.
Come out from among them, the lost."

House Left to Its Own
(A House Left to Its Own)

No respect? What do you expect?
No direction. Without God, no correction.
Life without discretion.
Going your own way day after day?
It's a home
Left to its own.

God must be the head.
If not, this home is dead.
In it there is no life.
Only strife.
Only God above can bring peace and love.
Without God it's push come to shove,
Backbiting,
Rioting.
The perfect atmosphere, enemy inviting.

For things to change,
Your life, you must choose to rearrange.
Choose God.
His path, trod.
Repent. Pray.

Speak the Word over your house today.
Speak victory over your house every day.
From God's Word, don't stray.
Love always.
Pray.

Humanity

For humanity all the works of thy flesh are vanity.
When thy day is done
Remember chance happeneth to everyone.
Whether it be good or bad, happy or sad,
Into judgment God will bring everything.
Repent. He shall redeem.

Man should fear God.
Do what He commands
According to God's plans.
For this is the whole duty of man.
He is able to make a stand.
If God be first, after righteousness thirst.
We have victory.
At Calvary Jesus says,
"You must come unto Me."

When God Chooses (God's Choice)

God doesn't look at us as a sinner.
He sees a winner!
He doesn't choose for us to lose.
God takes the used, abused and confused.
This is His plan,
Bringin man victorious to the Promised Land.

Go ahead and run from God if you will.
It's His plan: we must kneel.
God chooses whom He will.

It's your choice to listen to His voice.
It's not for us to reason how,
For every knee must bow.
He's choosing you,
So make the choice now.

A Double Minded Man
(Through the Word)

A double minded man is unstable in all his ways.
He must make up his mind.
See Jesus and peace He shall find.
All these things shall be added in God's time.
Through the Word, we take on Jesus mind.
The scales fall off our eyes. No longer blind.

Through the washing of the Word we are made whole.
And wisdom is better than gold,
Than a life of pleasure to behold.
Length of days God leading and guiding
And in Him abiding, being clothed in righteousness,
And from God, never hiding.
Only in Him, confiding.

I am bought and paid for through Jesus blood.

The Gift (This Gift)

A life lived in sin is a death sentence.
Thank you, Lord. You brought me to repentance.
You gave me this gift
So people's hearts I could lift.
This gift is Your voice,
So others can make their choice.

You give me inspiration. Correction.
You lead me in the right direction.
You gave me Your Word
So Your voice can be heard
To glorify You.
Your Word is true.
It brings salvation.
Restoration to all who will hear and draw near.

This gift speaks to the lost.
Count the cost.
Beckoning, come the way of the cross.
I cherish this gift, especially when I am weak
And when I hear You speak.
This gift is power unto salvation
Unto all generations.

Power of the Tongue

The power of the tongue,
We should learn while we are young.
What proceeds out of the mouth is what we become.

After the Word,
We should yearn, and it learn.
We should speak the Word aloud.
Let it be heard.

A good man's steps are ordered by the Lord.
If we live by the Word, God's voice will be heard.
Speaking life, we speak things into existence.
Through Him, we have assistance with no resistance.
Nothing is impossible with God.
Things can change in an instant.

Words

Words have power any hour.
You speak life or death.
What we speak always comes back.
That's fact.
I call heaven and earth to record.
In the Word there is no discord.
Only peace, joy, a sweet release.
Speaking life over your situation,
Over life's duration,
Brings victorious living.
A life of giving,
Adding life abundantly.
Blessings one can't contain.
Speaking Jesus is always the same.
Jesus is His Word,
So speak His name.

Thy Word

Thy Word I have hid in my heart,
Thy mercy and grace to never depart.
In Thy Word I have found pleasure
As I have found a hidden treasure,
For Thy Word has come unto me.
I have faith to see.

Though it was meant for my bad,
My heart is glad.
Thy Word is a lamp unto my feet.
I shall not suffer defeat.
In You, I am complete.

I've Anchored My Soul

I've anchored my soul in the Bible of old.
I've bought the truth. I shall sell it not.
Love, joy and peace I have got.
In Thy Word there are treasures untold,
Nuggets of gold.

To my Savior I'm sold out.
I have faith without doubt.
I shall leave this world with a shout,
Praising the Lord Jesus Christ as I go out!

The Season for Jesus

It's the season
For knowing Jesus is the reason.
It's a time for all mankind
For rejoicing in pleasing,
Opening our hearts to receiving.
Praising His name, our heritage.

Claim in the Spirit.
Taking hold in the Spirit of Christ, being bold,
Making sure the Christmas story is told.
Becoming part of the family of God,
Making sure with the Gospel our feet being shod.
All heaven and earth praising God.

The Good News

The Kingdom of heaven in near.
Let all speak God's Word and hear.
Hold the Word close, for it is dear.
It's the Good News. It doesn't abuse.
It's given for power in this day and hour
For you to use to become victorious, never to lose.

You can put a messed up life behind,
If Jesus Word you keep in mind.
The Word heals and sets free.
It brings love and victory
And a blessed life. You'll see.
Jesus says, "It's all through Me."

God Is in the Wind (God Is in...)

God is in the wind,
Sticking closer than a friend.
Sometimes blowing so strong,
Causing us to make sure our steps as we go along.

Putting our hand to the plow,
To the enemy never bow.
He is even in the cloud
And His strength is on us.
He begins to shroud.

Bringing us rain, washing a pain,
Taking away sin stain, making our way plain.
Bringing growth, everything turns green.

In the end, God does redeem.

Walking Along the Seashore

There was once a man walking along the seashore
Asking of God, "Give me more."
God said, "I stand at the door.
Knock. I am the Rock."
In Jesus name, write the vision.
Make it plain.
He wrote the vision in the sand.
There came a wave. Grand.
Not being able to stand,
Washing it away.

He began to pray.
He immersed himself out into the deep,
All heaven to rejoice, never to weep.
Being baptized in the Spirit,
Having his name written in the Lamb's book of life,
For eternity to keep.

Evening Rest

As the evening wanes,
The snow glistening over the plains.
As the sun recedes,
Watching the animals hunting for all their needs.
It's a beautiful sight just before it becomes night,
Realizing God made all things by the power of His might.
There is such a hush.
Everything is calm. No rush.
It's a time of reflecting
As the evening is directing.
Everything comes to a rest
As the moon begins to crest.
A time of knowing and thanking God for His best.

Down in the Valley

He maketh me to lie down in green pastures
Where, down in the valley, the beauty I see.
It's a place where Jesus has taken me.
It's a place of learning. No shadow of turning.
Pressing forward, no looking back.
Only for Jesus, yearning. Continually, learning.

Looking up,
The sides of the mountain arrayed with yellow and gold.
Such beauty to behold.
Skies strewn with clouds of white linen,
Life moving forward to a new beginning.
Oh, the awe of God.
At my heart, He doth prod.
Mountains of calm, rays of sunlight
At the breaking of daylight.
I stand in awe of my plight,
Realizing I can call on Him any day, any night,
Knowing He is in control.
And Satan can't devour. In Jesus, there is power!

My soul can be at rest
Down in the valley there is victory in life's test.
I'm now an overcomer and a Jesus runner.
I can have life's best!

A Planned Day
(An Encounter with the Heavenly Host)

I had planned out my day
But it didn't go that way.
Jesus talked to me.
He had plenty to say.
I encountered the Heavenly Host.
Yes, the Holy Ghost.

I'm walking through the heavenlies.
I can't describe what a wondrous site.
But I see Jesus in the power of His might!
The Most High God,
Letting me know where my feet hath trod,
Letting me know He is God!

So, I'm going about my day
In a much changed way.
Jesus is the Master of your day,
For He makes the way every day!

The Heart of Worship

It's all in the Sonship.
We must all come back to the heart of worship.
Have a longing to belonging,
To capture the heart of God.
Through His Word,
Planting our feet in His rich sod.

Seeking God's face
With patience, running the race.
From the start,
Seeking with our whole heart.

Knock, building on the solid rock.
Not seeking to please man,
Walk according to God's plan.
God being the center,
If heaven we want to enter.

Jesus, trust.
For Him, live with gust.

The Mortal Body

This mortal body of mine,
Given from the Divine.
Deterioration, sometimes lust, given to rust.
It is but sinful dust.

There is a plan for man:
Believing God. Born again,
Leading man to his Promised Land.

This mortal, taking on immortality, being risen,
Released from this fleshly prison.
Heirs of salvation,
Called by God from the creation.

The Times

There are times when people say, "I love you."
That's not how they really feel.
They aren't being real.
They're just being polite.
Somehow this doesn't seem right.
There are times people say they are your friend.
But in the end you find, on them you can't depend.
There are times you think this person, He just doesn't care.
He'll be the very one who'll be there.

There are times we think we're all alone.
Then we realize God's still on the throne.
There are times we feel like we can't go another mile!
Jesus speaks. He says, "You're my child."
He begins to refresh.
Reminds us we're but flesh
Made from the dust.
And in Him, we must trust.

There comes a time we realize to our demise.
God has been sending growing pains our way.
Reminds us that He's holding the reigns.

He still reigns.
There comes a time He reminds.
He's raising you up.
You've been drinking from the cup.
Yes, the cup of loneliness.
Sometimes being forsaken
And in your spirit feeling shaken.
Even being called a fool.
All the time God's been teaching you He does rule!

There comes a time in your heart
You realize You've taken part.
There comes a time in everyone's life God begins to heal the hurts
And says, "In you I've placed My seal."
The time will come You must come the way of the cross.
Because there was a time Jesus hung and died.
Rose again in victory for the lost.

There comes a time when Jesus says, "I'm a jealous God.
I'll have no other gods before me."
There'll come a time when Jesus will bring everything into light,

Reconciling all things unto Him where there's no more night.
There's come a time all things will be made new.
So when these things you go through,
Remember He's calling you!

Part 5: Prayer and Thanksgiving

Conversations with God

Conversations with God are good for the soul.
They never grow old, one's life story being told.

Recognizing God and His awesomeness in prayer.
Inviting Him in, Your burdens to share,
Realizing He is always there.

Omnipresent!
Omnipotent!
He's three in one,
Wrapped up in the Son!

In Him life began.
It's all in His plan.

In Him, forget not to communicate.
Conversations with God are the keys to enter Heaven's gate.
With Him, walk and talk.
Hear Him say, "In you I find no fault."

Sometimes (Sometimes I Say)

Sometimes I say,
"I'll go to church today."
Sometimes I say,
"I'm going to pray because I didn't do it yesterday."
Sometimes I say,
"I'm not going to commit sin."
But I do it again and again.

Sometimes I say,
"From now on I'm going to be kind."
But then I find that's not my state of mind.
Sometimes I say,
"I'm going to help people today."
But I find those were just thoughts of mine for the day.

Sometimes I say,
"I wonder why things never seem to go well for me?"
And then I think,
"Could it be because I didn't find time to pray each and every day?"

Sometimes I say,
"I just don't know which way to go."
And I think,
"Could this be because I didn't talk to Jesus?"

Sometimes I say,
"I really need to have a talk with Jesus anyway.
No matter what is going on in my life today.
I really need to pray
Because Jesus is the truth, the life and the way."
He is everything, at all times!

Communicate with God

Lord, in prayer You carefully take care.
You desire to communicate.
You're never late.
You're always ready to open the love gate.

Through prayer I can know Your will.
I only have to be still,
Knowing You are God.
With the Word, having my feet shod,
Giving me purpose in my walk.

Instant in season and out.
When I talk,
Never forgetting with You to communicate.
Prepares my way to enter the narrow gate,
Remembering prayer will get me there.

On Bended Knee

On bended knee I come to thee.
You comfort me.
Soon, with head bowed low
Your voice I come to know.

So gently speaking I can feel Your hands reaching
Gently, but firmly taking hold.
Soon Your glory I behold,
Engulfing my soul, speaking things that can't be uttered by word.
But You are heard,
Engulfed by the Holy Ghost.

I have been visited by the Heavenly host.
Taking my hand, lifting me up that I may stand.
The weight is all gone,
For I know I'm not alone.
I'm certain to whom I belong.

Teaching me there will be valleys and mountains high.
All I need is to speak Your name.
You are always nigh.
You regard me as the apple of Thine eye.

I Come in Prayer

Lord, I come to You in prayer.
I know You're there
With an everlasting care.
When I'm on my knees
I find I'm looking up.
You fill my cup.
With You I sup.

When I'm down and my troubles abound,
I find You're always around.
You lift me high, comforting.
You're always nigh.
You cannot lie.

You direct my path
So I won't suffer wrath.
You set angels over me,
Opening my eyes that I might see,
Prayerfully.

Seeking God (A Prayer to Begin Today)

Lord, light my way
As I begin today.
Give me eyes that I might see
What You want me to be.

Guide my steps
And keep my lips from speaking ill.
Speaking life, never death to kill.
Guide my hands swiftly from wrong,
Touching my lips with song.

Let me encourage those that are down,
Giving a smile instead of a frown.
But most of all Lord, put me in one mind and one accord.
Always in word or deed, seeking the Lord.

Seek God

Make a decision.
Be Spirit driven.
Seek God first,
As though you were dying of thirst.
Seek His life-giving blood
When the enemy comes in like a flood.
Give your all.
Seek the Savior's call.

Find Your place.
Run this race.
Insecurity and jealousy will flee.
Covered by His blood,
They have no more power over thee.

Reach out.
Take His hand.
He's seeking such throughout the land.

My Tears

Sometimes I can't find the words to say.
Can't pray.
But my tears find the way

From the depth of my soul
Jesus meets my tears and does console.
He understands,
Reaches out His hands.
No words are spoken, just being broken.
Emptying my heart to the Master who is in control.

Me, He beings to console,
Letting me know
He knows the plans He has for me.

Can't find the words to pray.
Weary and tired, seemingly lost my way.
Weary and tired.

Press On

Press on and pray through the Word,
Doing things His way.

Too often we settle for less.
We stress.
This shouldn't be.
We should bend our knee.
Pray every day.

Don't succumb.
Overcome,
Calling on Jesus name!
His Word, claim.
Proclaim Jesus the same!
Then we can soar,
Have what Jesus has in store.
The high calling, overcoming power.
This day and hour!

Pray One for Another

You've heard,
"He ain't heavy. He's my brother."
In prayer,
We should pray one for another!

Lifting the heavy hands that hang down,
Reminding them eternal life can be found.
Speaking the Word in due season.
To God, be pleasing.

Lord Grant Me

Lord, to others let me be a light.
Give me the will to do what is right in Your sight.
To walk in the Spirit, not by might.
In the Spirit, fight the good fight,
Reminding the enemy his plight.

Lord, grant me discernment,
Not looking on the outward appearance.
In You, reverence,
Discerning what is right and wrong,
Knowing to You I belong.

Lord, give me a heart.
And from You, never to depart,
Reminding others they too can have a new start.
A life on You, depending.
Life with no ending

More of You

Lord, give me more of You.
Make my life anew.
To you, be sold out,
Without a doubt.
Let me leave this world with a shout,
Being called out.

If I should stumble put a guard over my lips.
Never to grumble.
Given to repent,
Knowing I have been sent.
Spreading the Word where it can be heard.

Don't let me live a life of shame.
Whatever I do in word or deed,
To Your word, taking heed.
Doing it in Your name,
Let my life henceforth be pleasing in Your sight.
Walking in the Spirit, in the power of Your might!
Lord, let this be my plight,

Doing right in Your sight.
Never let me live to please man.
Let me live according to Your plan.
Give me faith to say, "I can!"
In the end, for You stand.

A Time of Thanksgiving

Thanksgiving is a time for thankful living.
Thankful for blessings from on high.
A time for God and family to draw nigh.
A time of reflection.
A time of personal correction.
A time of sound direction.
It's a time for enjoying family and friends.
It's a time when the festivities begin,
Thanking God for everything.
A time of joy. A time to sing!

Thankfulness makes one's heart well.
It's good for the spirit. One can tell.
Soon you can tread through life, even sail.
And through much You shall prevail.

God's Plan My Mother (God's Plan)

God gave me my mother.
I would discover I have no other.
All the days of my life I have been in God's hands.
He has brought me to understand.
He has made me perfect in His sight,
Teaching me righteous living,
Leading me to His glorious light.

My mother gave me birth,
But living for God gives me worth.
For of Him and through Him and to Him are all things.
To Him be glory forever, whatever this life brings.
So glory to God in the highest,
My heart sings!

Part 6: Life, Now and to Come

Such a Gift (A Gift of God)

A gift God sent
When the night was almost spent.
But such a gift God did send.
Eternal life without end.

In the eastern sky that night,
The star did shine so bright
In the power of His might,
As God's plan was in plain sight
Reconciling the world, making everything right.

A Savior in human flesh,
Bringing man with right standing with God.
A gift to keep. A call to us all.
God, seek.

New Life

Those without your memories
Can't understand your pain.
They can't relate the same.
God sees your tears
You've cried over the years.
Your eyes, He clears,
Bringing joy through your pain.
Wisdom and understanding to gain,
Through forgiveness of the sin, letting Jesus in.
A new life will begin
And Him calling us friend
In a world without end.

A New Song

I'm marching to a new song.
Singing to Jesus, to whom I belong.
It's the song of victory. A victorious bride.
He's changing me on the inside.

I'm making a stand.
Going to live according to God's plan.

He called me by my name.
Said He took on Himself my shame.
He's taking away all blame,
If in Him I would live.
To me, eternal life He will give.

I'm marching to a new song.
He's preparing me an eternal home.
And with Him, I will live.
To me, eternal life He will give.

Rich in Jesus (Living for Jesus)

Living for Jesus I have become rich,
For He has delivered by soul from the ditch.
In Him, my tent I have pitched.
I am rich in love straight from heaven's realm.

It's a heavenly sound
When Jesus You hang around.
I'm drunk on His Spirit.
Full of His wine.
I'm drinking from the One True Vine.
I'm living for Jesus.
I can hear Him say, "Thou art mine."

I'm walking through the heavenlies.
I can't describe what a wondrous site.
I can see Jesus in the power of His might.

Did you hear me?
My eyes are wide open.
They're not shut.
In the Spirit I'm caught up as heaven sings.
It's like nothing living in the flesh brings.

As my heart is pounding
I can hear His trumpet sounding
And His love is abounding.
In Him, I'm rich!

This World Is Not My Home

This world is not my home.
I'm a foreigner following Jesus. I'm not alone.
I'm not afraid nor dismayed, to question my Savior
No man can persuade.
My eyes are on the prize.
I know my demise.
I am a child of the King.
To heaven I am bound.

I now sing, "Jesus is my everything."
He's all I need. He's all I need!
He gave His life for me. He did bleed.
Covered by His blood and forgiven,
I know my Savior has risen.

He's leading and guiding me to heaven my home.
Never more to roam,
Where loved ones I'm going to see
And be part of God's family.
I now shout with glee! Jesus, I shall see.
Jesus love doth cover me into eternity.

My New Home

I'm moving to my new home.
I'm going to set up residence, no more to roam.
My walls are decorated with scenes of love.
My foundation is built from above.
My windows are clear
Because I'll keep Jesus near.
In prayer, I'll plant me a garden.
In remembrance, my sins Jesus did pardon.

It'll be a home of compassion,
Hospitality without ration.
A place to rest, building it to my very best.
Not a place of jest.
Consecrated to my Savior,
A home of prayer built with must care.
I'll sweep out the dust
And remember Jesus, to trust.
Remembering, He gave me my home
And, most of all, I'm never alone
Because Jesus is on the throne.
And He resides in my new home.

Thinking on Salvation (My Eternal Home)

Thinking on my salvation
And the duration of the destination,
How God in creation had a plan for man.
I'm excited about the journey to my eternal home,
Never more to be alone, never more to roam.
I'll see God around that great white throne.
There'll be streets of gold and no more night.

I will have fought the good fight,
Understanding salvation is not by might
But by God's Spirit, knowing those who worship God
Must worship Him in Spirit and in truth.
To enter in and turn from sin,
Believing He is and a rewarder of them that diligently seek Him.
Knowing He is the I am, the Alpha and the Omega,
The Beginning and the End.

The Prodigal Comes Home

Like the prodigal son, when the day is done
We must realize we're not alone.
We must make our journey home.
No more going our own way.
Come home to stay.
Our Father in heaven awaits
With open arms, us to embrace.
Even giving the ultimate sacrifice of His only Son,
Taking our place.
Atoning for our sin, so heaven we could enter in.
We must abide. Enter in.

Come inside. In Jesus, hide.
Receiving our inheritance, obtaining our riches in glory,
Obtaining eternal life. The end of the story!

A Thing That Is Bad
(God Has Prepared a Place)

Sometimes a thing that is bad
Can make you want to give in to being sad.
But to the feet of them having their feet shod
With the preparation of the Gospel, should be glad.
For God has prepared a place
Where men can look on His redeemer's face
And rest from this fleshly race.
Then, God Himself will embrace:
"Welcome home. Come live in this place."

There'll be no more tears.
No fears. Endless years,
No more to count. No more night.
No more fight, only walking in the light,
Living in the power of God's might where there is pure white.
White as snow.
God's saving power you will know
And all things to you He'll show.

When I Get to Heaven

When I get to heaven
I'll stand in God's glorious bright light.
There'll be no more darkness.
There'll be no more night.
I'll be singing and shouting God's praise
For leading and guiding all of my days,
Him showing me His faithful ways.
Giving me the chance to run this race.
Finally, to see His face
In the light of His mercy and grace
In that great glorious place.

I will shout and sing, letting the praises ring.
He's the King of Kings!
What a glorious day that will be.
My eyes will finally be open: His full glory.
I will see what He has made of me,
For I have gone out into eternity

I've Gone Home

Don't weep for me.
Give God glory,
For my life tells the story.
I've had a long life here on earth.
Now I've gone on to a new birth.
Jesus has welcomed me home.
I'm not alone.
I have no more tears.
I've gained endless years,
Being with Jesus and angels, too,
Not to mention life anew.

Just think of me as being on vacation,
One of a long destination.
I'm now in the company of the great cloud of witnesses
Singing and praising God, in whom I have believed.
My soul is now relieved.
Just know I love you all.
I heard Jesus call.
It was time for me to go home.

I now live in a beautiful place.
I now see Jesus face to face.

Call Me Gone

Call me gone!
I'm headed to my eternal home,
That city not made with hands
Where there are angel bands
Singing around God's throne.
Never more to be alone.
No more dying, the sting of death defying.
No more putting up with lying.
No more tears, but length of years without end.
Jesus calling me friend.
What a joyous jubilee for my family and me!
No more destruction. No more corruption
Going to sit down and talk to my friend.
Conversation without end.

I'm Building a City

I'm building a city.
Come run this race.
I'm building a city."
Gonna look on Jesus' face.
I'm building a city
Not made with hands.
I'm building a city.
I'm loosing the bands.
I'm building a city
With vast treasures untold.
I'm building a city,
My glory to behold.
I'm building a city
Not to be sold.
I'm building a city
Built on love.
I'm building a city.
It's a home up above.

Part 7: Words from God

God Spoke

One day I heard God call my name.
He took away the pain.
He spoke plain: "Follow me.
You'll never be the same.
You are now a part of the family of God.

I'll lead and guide.
In My house, abide.
I have many gifts to install.
Turn to Me.
Give Me your will.
On you I have placed My seal.
Eternal life is real."

Love, God.

My People

My people, who are called by My name:
Come out of the wilderness.
Come out of the night.
Step into the light.

I am cleaning, redeeming, sweeping the land.
Everything must bow at My command.
I am coming in the power of My right hand.
Restoring, evil abhorring by My demand.
My Word shall stand forever.
Endeavor for the faith. Don't waiver,
For I am your Savior.

I heal and make whole.
I will give back what the enemy stole.
I am He before days of old.
I shape and mold.
The future, I hold.
My Word is a lamp unto your feet.
Come. My face, behold.
Eat and drink of Me. I set free.
I'm calling My bride.
Come unto Me.

Follow Me

My ways are perfect, tried and true.
In My Word did I not say I will never leave
nor forsake you?
My mercy endures to the end.
This you can depend.

I delight in the praises of My people.
Never looking upon fine steeples, I love a humble heart.
This is rich ground, My gifts to impart.
I promise a continual feast and long length of days
If you would but only heed My ways.
Lean on me. Again, I say lean.

In this life there will be many troubles.
Sometimes it comes in double.
In Me, put your trust.
Remember, have faith. This you must.
Put away all lying.
Remember sin is only for the dying.
I promise life without end.
Remember, I control the wind.
Keep your eyes on the prize.

Stay in the Word. In Me, be wise.
Pray every day.
I promise you will be heard.
I'll never suffer your foot to stumble.
I resist the proud and give ear to the humble.
So gird up your mind.
I promise Jesus, you can find.
In Me life is not hard.
Only to the sinner.
Follow Me. I've won.
Be the winner.

Know That I Am God

Be still where thy feet doth trod.
Be still. Know that I Am God.
For thou art on holy ground
Wherever I Am found.
You have found grace.
Behold you shall see My face. So, taste.

See that I Am good.
I would that none should perish.
My Word, cherish.
Keep your heart pure.
You can rest assured
I Am the King of Kings!
I Am All in All.
The living water from life's well-springs.
Be complete in Me.
Have all that life brings.

I knew you before time.
You are mine.
I know you by name.
I never change.

I'm always the same.
Be still. Know that I Am God
No matter where thy feet trod.

I Made Everything

I made everything.
Made the birds to sing.
It's no small thing.
In My image I created man.
It's all in My plan.
Be encouraged, never discouraged.

I knew you before you were born.
You, I formed. You, I adorned.
I created you in the image of your Father.
In His image He created you.
Can't you see you have His ways, too?
He's an example to pursue.
You can do more than He could ever do.

I say set your sights high.
To Me, come nigh.
The enemy can't defeat. You shall defy.
Keep a single eye.
It is I, saith God.

With the Gospel, keep your feet shod.
All will come into place if you will seek My face.
I'll bring everything into perspective,
Everything into its right place.
I want to bless. In Me, rest.
Ask. For Me, it's no task.
Try Me, saith God.
Living for Me can be a blast.
I do a quick work, fast.
I am He.
Come follow Me.

I Will

I will lead you and guide you,
I will. I am the Word and the Truth.
I will hide you in the shadow of My wings.
I will teach you all things.
I will be with you in the darkest of night.
I will put the enemy to flight.
I will bring every work into the light.
I will see.
I will speak to the weak.
I will promised blessed assurance.
I will cause endurance.
I will be a friend.
I will. I am even unto the end.

Pray

Pray every day.
And yet, while you are still speaking, I will hear.
I will gird you up. I am near.

Come to Me in prayer.
Your thoughts with Me, share.
Prayer is where you will find rest
And life at its best.
Strength for your soul,
I've promised since days of old.
In My house there are many mansions.
So be My guest and your soul shall find rest.

Prayer and praise is where I am found,
And My love does abound.
Prayer and faith turn things around.
There is life found in prayer.

Tell Them

Tell them I died, rose again.
Conquered death, hell and the grave to set men free.
Tell them, I am He.
Tell them again, to the cross I would go.
Tell them I am love. I love them so.
Tell them I would that none should perish.
Tell them I am love. I cherish.
Tell them I am everything they need!
Tell them I gave all for them. I did bleed.
Tell them I gave My life's blood.
Tell them eternal life came in like a flood.
Tell them it's for whosoever will.
Tell them come as you are. I love the sinner still.
Tell them the enemy comes but to kill and steal.
Tell them I bind up the broken hearted. I heal.
Tell them I break the yoke.
Tell them I spoke.

Steal No More

To him who stole, steal no more.
It will only make you poor,
For I know what you have need of.
I look upon thee from above.
Before you ask I'm ready to give,
If for Me you live.

Look at Me.
You'll see I'll take care of thee.
I formed thee from the dust.
In Me, trust.
After worldly things, don't lust.
Keep your eyes on Me.
Live eternally.

Take Back

I employ.
The thief cometh not but to kill, steal and destroy.
I've given you power this day and hour!

Take back.
Suffer no lack.
It is I.
I shall supply.

In Me, pursue the enemy.
Subdue.
Fast and pray.
It's the only way.
Give Me your all today.

Take back what the enemy has stole.
Seek Me.
I heal.
I give back. I don't steal.
From sin, turn.
For My children I yearn.
Come unto Me.
I set free.

Run the Race

Come the way of the cross.
Don't suffer loss.
I am the truth, the life, and the way.
Work while it is still day.
I would that none should be lost.
Count the cost.
Forgive, live and give!

Seek ye first the kingdom of God.
I prepare the way in which thy feet trod.
Love thine enemy and do good.
Pick up the cross and follow Me. Do as I would.
Take no thought for food and raiment.
I shall supply for you are the apple of Mine eye.
Choose life. Refuse strife.
Let thine eye be single.
With sin, don't mingle.
Let thine whole body be full of light,
Full of the Spirit, full of God's might!
Run the race. Fight the fight.
See God face to face!

Welcome Home Child of Mine

Welcome home child of Mine.
You're a branch from the true vine.
I've been calling, 'Come home,' oh for so long.
Welcome back. It's as if you had never been gone.

I beseech. I'm a restorer of the breach.
So I say reach!
Yes, reach out for Me.
I'll show you things you never thought you would see.
Seek and keep your heart meek.
Eye hath no seen. Ear hath not heard.
Neither has it entered into the heart of man.
Have faith! You can stand.

There are treasures in My Word.
So stay close to the heavenly host.
I'm turning your life around.
Attend unto My Words.
They are life.
My doctrine is sound.
I can always be found.
You only need to call.

I won't let you fall.
I'll always be around.
I never leave nor forsake.

So, look up.
Your redemption draweth nigh,
For you're the apple of My eye.
Yes, peace I have prepared
And My Word have declared.

www.ingramcontent.com/pod-product-compliance
Lightning Source LLC
Chambersburg PA
CBHW060529100426
42743CB00009B/1468